SHEARSMAN
105 & 106

WINTER 2015 / 2016

GUEST EDITOR, ISSUE 105 / 106
KELVIN CORCORAN

EDITOR
TONY FRAZER

This issue is dedicated to the memory of

Lee Harwood

(6 June 1939 – 26 July 2015)

Shearsman magazine is published in the United Kingdom by
Shearsman Books Ltd
50 Westons Hill Drive | Emersons Green | BRISTOL BS16 7DF

Registered office: 30-31 St James Place, Mangotsfield, Bristol BS16 9JB
(this address not for correspondence)

www. shearsman.com

ISBN 978-1-84861-446-8
ISSN 0260-8049

This compilation copyright © Shearsman Books Ltd., 2015.
All rights in the works printed here revert to their authors, translators or original copyright-holders after publication. Permissions requests may be directed to *Shearsman*, but they will be forwarded to the copyright-holders.

Subscriptions and single copies

Current subscriptions—covering two double-issues, with an average length of 108 pages—cost £14 for delivery to U.K. addresses, £17 for the rest of Europe (including the Republic of Ireland), and £19 for the rest of the world. Longer subscriptions may be had for a pro-rata higher payment. North American customers will find that buying single copies from online retailers in the U.S.A. will often be cheaper than subscribing. The reason is that airmail postage rates in the U.K. have risen rapidly, whereas copies of the magazine are printed in the U.S.A. to meet demand from online retailers there, and thus avoid the transatlantic journey.

Back issues from nº 63 onwards (uniform with this issue) cost £8.50 / $14 through retail outlets. Single copies can be ordered for £8.50 direct from the press, post-free in the U.K., through the Shearsman Books online store, or from any bookshop.
Issues of the previous pamphlet-style version of the magazine, from nº 1 to nº 62, may be had for £3 each, direct from the press, where copies are still available, but contact us for a quote for a full, or partial, run.

Submissions

Shearsman operates a submissions-window system, whereby submissions are only accepted during the months of March and September, when selections are made for the October and April issues, respectively. Submissions may be sent by mail or email, but email attachments—other than PDFs—are not accepted.
We aim to respond within 3 months of the window's closure.

Acknowledgements

The translations of Winétt de Rokha in this issue are published by kind permission of Patricia Tagle, acting for the author's Estate.

Contents

Lee Harwood	4
Peter Riley	5
Carmen Bugan	9
Clayton Eshleman	14
Donna Stonecipher	19
Tamar Yoseloff	22
Philip Terry	24
Astrid Alben	29
Amy Wright	32
Janet Sutherland	35
Samir Guglani	38
Helen Tookey	42
Ian Davidson	45
Sabiyha Rasheed	49
Dorothy Lehane	52
Ian Seed	55
Claire Crowther	58
David Miller	61
Jaime Robles	63
Juana Adcock	66
Helen Moore	70
Gerrie Fellows	74
Aidan Semmens	77
Lucy Sheerman	81
Lucy Hamilton	84
Mark Dickinson	86
Elżbieta Wójcik-Leese	91

Marina Tsvetaeva *(translated from Russian by Angela Livingstone)* 94
Philippe Jaccottet   *(translated from French by Ian Brinton)*   97
Winétt de Rokha   *(translated from Spanish by J. Mark Smith)*   98
Osip Mandelstam   *(translated from Russian by Alistair Noon)* 101

Biographical Notes   103

Lee Harwood

Philatelic Counter

Homage to Donald Evans 1945-1977

A Post Office van is parked by the roadside
in an imaginary country.
We can imagine the postman trudge up a grassy track
to deliver letters and a packet to a remote cottage.

We can imagine the stamps printed in washed-out magenta
or a faded dark blue or light ochre. Maybe many years ago.
A series of stamps portraying heroic deeds
in this country's history, or flowers of the meadow.

What a comfort this world is.
But even here there are people who really disappear,
go away, or simply die and are buried in a green meadow.
The fire swept through the building, nothing was saved.

What's in those letters?
Waiting for news, or reminders of what matters.
To be clear – not too easy – about what next,
not just drifting back and forth carried by accident.

In what seems a vision it's as though
an untouched snowfield lies in front of us.
Anything could be possible.
There's a glitter in the air as we head out.

The silver darkens on the ikon as the year ends.
Time to get out the silver polish!
and a soft cotton cloth.
Come spring a grove of almond trees turns white with blossom.

The Post Office van drives off leaving two muddy ruts.

Peter Riley

On Islands

(i) Bardsey

You walk above in the light
on soft ground, creatures of thought
glowing off the sea and the distance
to be gained. Haze on the fields
spreading upwards.

What we do here: live, more days,
climbing the stairs to the bed-loft each night
and lying there, waiting for
events in the sky. On the morning window-ledge
sunlight falls through a seagull's wing.

Days and nights of wind and bird sound
the sea pushing its lines towards the land
a hundred and twenty-one seals in the bay.
And out of all this a speaking to a purpose
out of this a reciprocal song.

Saints buried under the track, streaks
of limestone in the grass. Who went
unrecorded, whose being lives
somewhere else, far away, Doncaster
or Freetown, in acts of heartedness.

Strange birds fill the night with cackling
and squeaking over our thin roof. We lie
in the loft trying not to sleep until the sky

is quiet again, dream components
drifting towards the island.

The birds are Manx shearwater and they
know their tunes by heart all over the night.
The form of thought that they represent
mentions global fidelity and the price
of groceries at this time of year.

Massed voices from the sea, statements about the world
in scribbled notes blown out of the hand, lost in the wind
found again in a book or a bone flute. Decked
in red and white bands the unmanned lighthouse
attracts migrating birds to their death at night.

To stay and get older, learning the details, of sea currents,
cloud formations, whereabouts of the hut circles on the hill.
And to sit on the bench against the harbour shed
in late sunshine watching the lobster boat coming in,
without candy floss, without writers in residence.

To stay and get older day by day as the
mind quickens to the task and acts
of judgement become acts of justice.
How does this happen? By what principle
as delicately toned as a blackbird's egg.

Salt corroded iron ring in a stone stump,
bright red. Cist burials in the shoreline bank.
Catch my breath before it blows away. Trust
the principle. Leave the door unlocked all night.
Only the sea breeze will visit. Be sure to vote.

Alert at night in the loft, free of the eyes' commands
breathing like sleeping babies, thoughts always open,
always clear, thoughts you bring with you,
language that pursues you and here
come those crazy birds again.

We lie here and things happen
elsewhere, nothing can stop them.
Guilt dated 1945 and more massacres.
A voice is nothing unless appointed.
Sea murmuring and hissing grass,

There is no voice. There is no sense of.
The sea's eyes are closed under the soles
of your thought, year after year inching the self
towards a question to be asked about what is shared.
Wind. Birdsong. Death Stones.

That's no answer. There is no answer.
There is no silence. Listen to the mad
cacophony of the shearwater, making
species calls to their young all night,
island night, is it you are you there?

When day comes, listen. Listen
to the grass. Listen to the gravestones.
There is a whispering about the isle
that delights and harms not,
clearest at night, when the mind takes its part

And clear in the day when it rains.
Look it up in a dictionary, write
to the newspapers, tell us the facts,

getting older, moving slowly,
all comfort beyond.

This word and that and some others
and I sense an approaching proposition
creeping here under cover of night,
but everything I think is interrupted
by two thousand rubber ducks in the sky.

Creatures of thought, raging in the night sky
stamping your syllables into the soil
from which emerge baby birds and fly away
over thousands of miles of ocean bearing thoughts
that all may yet be the best it can.

Carmen Bugan

The House Founded on Elsewhere

He who turns against his language, adopting that of others, changes his identity and even his deceptions. He tears himself—a heroic betrayal—from his own memories, and up to a point, from himself.
—Emil Cioran, from *The Temptation to Exist*
(*translated from Romanian by Carmen Bugan*)

I.

Today is allowed to exist and then vanish
Like the seagulls and their shadows on
The still-seeming water in the Bay of Bantry,

Where I walk unnoticed, unrecorded,
Making memories of compass jellyfish swimming
Up with the tide, after the storm, to the beach.

My own shadow, stooping, standing
Over rocks and sand, back on the walking path
Simply means that I exist, and there is light.

That is all that will remain of today, no official record
Will testify against what I say that I see. As for me,
I hover in the space between the seagull and its shadow

Loose like a thought that tries to cling to something,
To celebrate the swans and their mirror image,
That medusa that opens like a flower in the sun,

Green lobster nets and masts of boats
Writing something oracular on the horizon
For those who are without a home.

II.

The first crack appeared on the ceiling:
Thin like the shadow of a spider's thread
Cast along the crease where the walls merge.

No one other than her noticed it there.
She couldn't take her mind off it, the way it
Stood in her view as she looked out at mountains

Between trees from her place at the table:
It brought a subtle wrinkle on her face.
Later on a larger fissure appeared, the paint

Swelled like the skin below the eye following
Sleepless nights, plain to see above the table.
She set to mixing cement, took out

Smoothing instruments, drained the weeping wall
And mended until all looked well again.
She built the new house with words bought

At the price of exile, letting memories go astray,
Fall where they may like dust.
How many times she walked around her house

Anxious and proud that she made it all with a translated
Prayer, a new version of the old prayer, holy
Oil from elsewhere, rituals and superstitions

From elsewhere, but all renewed and changed
Again, four languages over, where they show
Why they could pass through words that changed her.

III.

When the walls became full of cracks she knew no words
She cemented would last unless she uncovered
The foundation of elsewhere on which her house was built.

She dug around it, moved the earth little by little until the old stones
Showed through: porous pain, old fears, mistrust. She placed
Next to them what she could find around: a bit of happiness, a bit
    of fear

A little bit of courage. All in the language where she
She learned them. Cement now, water, patience,
Piece by piece the foundation is renewed.

She looks at her children and husband. She will mend this wall
With words from here and elsewhere and let them
Help her build, rebuild and fix: their common love and skill

Should outlast time, be stronger than her will alone.
They play-build like when she was young and poured the foundation
Of that first house she cannot forget: the childhood house of joy.

IV.

Stefano is three years old, he fills his shirt with pears
And runs: 'Mommy look, what shall we do with them?'
I take out the camera and rush to him, his soft cheeks,
Busy little hands, his golden curls. The grass is full of pears.

V.

Alisa puts her arms around me: 'Come play with me',
She runs around the room with her bare little feet, here, there,
Like a sunray that escapes through wind-blown trees
In summer's day and lights up unexpected places.

VI.

It is the lucid sky after the wind
Has swept the debris that has come from far away:

Cirrus clouds like torn night shirts,
On the shoulder of the Jura whitened with first snow.

All clean now wherever you look, lit by the coin of the moon.
Turning to the second half of life,

Knees grazed against the web of splintered light.
And here it comes, a word at work through those fallen notes:

The touch that brings on all other touches
With the rightness in them, turning and moving again with you

The moonlight sonata in my ears in morning sun at the desk:
Different this time, a new kind of music, awake, luminous.

VII.

Not all the words you say are the Self and not all turning
Against your language is self-betrayal. Behind each word
Is what tries to get inside it. That is what matters

Whether I speak it in my own language
Or in the tongue of others. The thought, the breath
With which you send love out, or forgiveness, say,

Outlive the words and languages, outstrip
The syllables at prayer or play. I speak of smiles and tears
And better yet, smiles through tears at the end of day.

And so the house stands with what it can:
A sagging wall, a brand new door through which
Come children with schoolbooks and street-side flowers;

Solid enough to face the winter wind and baking heat,
Each word inside for what it's worth and what it can say:
Good enough to bear the weight of what's to come.

June 18 – July 10, 2014

Clayton Eshleman

The Dream's Navel

For Stuart Kendall

Gotham Bar & Grill in Manhattan, dining with Caryl, Cecilia & Jim.
At a table near ours, alone, a woman in whose face I saw Death.
At one point she turned her head toward us:
I could only stay in her *black ray lane* a few seconds.

So, here we are. Sipping cheek timber, under the cistern eyes of earth's granite-gated vineyard.

Cecilia Vicuña: the shadow
    is from the animal
    you used to be
    the shadow
    is from the one
    you will be
    the shadow is not from you
    from them
    from the one who passes
    its not a shadow at all
    it is the sound
    of a shadow
    it is the shadow
    of the sound"

Freud: "There is a tangle of dream thoughts that cannot be unraveled. This is the dream's navel, the spot where it reaches down into the unknown."

Or as rephrased by Freud: "There is at least one spot in every dream at which it is unplumbable—a navel as it were, that is its point of contact with the unknown."

Freud also identifies the dream navel as a knot entangled with threads (evoking the Medusa's head of serpent hair covering the mother's "dangerous genitals"). He writes that some "dream thoughts are infinitely branching, rather than tangled…"

At one point he identifies the dream navel with the defile, or central neck, of a clepsydra, "where all forms resemble each other, where everything is possible."

The spot where this navel "reaches down into the unknown," can be envisioned as an Upper Paleolithic opening leading to a cave, the maternal interior being replaced by a limestone one; the "infinitely branching thoughts" becoming the engraved meanders on Rouffignac's "Red Ceiling with Serpentines," a surface covered with serpent-shaped signs.

Or as in Combarelle's Inner Gallery, the engraved creatures that only vaguely resemble anything that lived:
        animal-snouted archaic on the leash of,
        or the harness of, a proto-alchemical mush,
        sled beasts bounding in slow motion,
        grotesque heads dissolving in grotto drift…

Can these silex-cut wall meanders and lines or black manganese finger strokes, unreadable but engageable, indicate a possible response of Cro-Magnon people in cave darkness to a dream's branchings & grotesque inhabitants? Can we cut through time here and descend, without historical interference, through the palimpsestic layers of unconscious levels, to uncover the possible ignition of image making, in which non-human souls began to mingle with human souls?

"In fact," Gaston Bachelard proposes, "a need to animalize is at the origins of the imagination… its first function is to create animal forms."

Henri Michaux's stroke chaos, in which creature forms are evoked by tangled and knotted lines reminds us of the Cro-Magnon

"creatures" verging on resembling something living, yet undefined...
As if we are in the presence of nothing in the process of becoming...

Vicuña again: "The void, the forgotten aspect of each sound that is propelling us as we search for memory and oblivion at once..."

One day I will be between here & there, in the nowhere that is part of every where that tonight seems substantial compared to its invisible absence...

My absence... as if absence were mine.

Old Whitman: "Have you learn'd lessons only of those who admired you, and were tender with you, and stood aside for you? Have you not learn'd great lessons from those who reject you, and brace themselves against you? Or who treat you with contempt, or dispute the passage with you?"

Willliam & Cid,
with you I've lived.
Corman said no
& Blake said yes.

We are free only to the degree that we are able to acknowledge the headless oarsmen rowing the heart skiff through the rainbow of a
        totality
ebbing & flowing over
the rocks of man's now quite clearly unregenerate nature.

We have lost the *temenos*, the imaginative precinct
    in which van Eyck, say,
could orchestrate a specific world

Dearth of polar bears. Dearth of honeybees.

        It is crying outside.

*

    Image is the athanor in which I linguistize soul,
a dream umbilicus coiling down into the miracle of
Neanderthal tombstone cupules, Cro-Magnon engravings,
    earliest shamanic hybrids,
        through which a mistress spirit might rise,
electric with Tantrik lesions, from that serpent lounge
where the soul snake slumbers
until charmed up into a brain / body imaginarium.

My mind at base is a spermal animalcule
impregnated with female blood.
The Muladhara Chakra is not gendered
    nor is my imagination.
I reject duality & propose an orgy of contesting mind.
The soul was in exile even at Chauvet.

Paradise is a form of polymorphous merger
charged by the bathysphere of the poem
rising from engrailings where even squirrels reflect,
& robins ruminate: the animal lager…

        Bottom is crossed by
something alive, a crab or turtle brought up mud
regurgitated into a Cro-Magnon hand.
Ochre or manganese, discovered in descent
& mixed with cave water, palm pressed to stone
(a stone that in history becomes the omphalos, or om phallus),
released, leaving a "hand" without a hand,
negation's—or was it absence's?—first
        imaginal presence.

The poem is from the beginning antiphonal
hybridizing ancestral fauna in language-twisted straits.
Oh the difficulty of the soul! "You could not find the ends of the soul
though you traveled every way, so deep is its logos."
To Heraclitus, James Hillman responds: "the logos of the soul,
Psychology, implies the act of traveling the soul's labyrinth
in which *we can never go deep enough.*"

William Blake, naked, reading Genesis to naked Catherine
in their London "Arbor of Eden."

Jardin botanique, Bordeaux, 2008.
The bud & spoor density of a mauve Baudelairian incubation.
Tender vines erupting into fanged blooms...
Minute nomadic ants percolate the many-breasted
    Venus of the Plants.
Centuries pass... And the ghost of Henri Rousseau
        glides,   a virgin on a lost ark,
        in chime with cloned obsequies,
            fertile diapasons...

Fused to his centrovertic grappling,
into the aethercore the poet pours his siliceous soul.

Donna Stonecipher

Snow Series 2

     There once was a polar bear who didn't know that he was a polar bear, because he'd been raised in a zoo by people. What would a polar bear have to know, to know that he was a polar bear? That's what the people would never know. All that winter, as we wandered around town, we kept noticing how the segmented bodies of snowmen resembled those of ants', and how the new snow resembled other, older snows.

*

     The beautiful young woman slowly realized that her beauty was a currency, but did not know how to spend it. "It is difficult to be beautiful for long" wrote Max Jacob. The young woman read this and forgot it. The Swiss chalets dotting the hillside resembled other Swiss chalets. The polar bear who didn't know that he was a polar bear had snowy fur reflecting those regions where only our supercooled minds can go.

You were the one who wanted to ride the télépherique all day long that winter, to float up over the Alps and then back down into the valley in an endless paternoster loop that would keep cycling us in and out of the sweetest ether. If "architecture is frozen music," then "music" must be "liquid architecture." The architecture itself was frozen: there were chalets trapped in aspics of ice. There were ants frozen in icicles.

*

In another city, people flocked to the zoo to imagine owning a baby polar bear named Flocke, whom they would relinquish to her fate once she grew out of the phase in which they wished to crush her snowy soft fur with bear hugs. "Flocke" means "snowflake." The wonder of uniqueness. No two snowflakes are alike, like no two humans. Unique snowflakes exploded on our tongues. The wonder of ownership.

Wonder upon wonder, snowy Alp upon snowy Alp upon snowy Alp. One Alp resembled another Alp. No two polar bears are alike. Gliding up and up on the télépherique, we felt we were at last one with the Alps: encased in a glass eye floating up over the snow, all eye ourselves, our bodies architectonically segmented into distance, ownership, and desire. The glacier below us was beautiful, beautifully, violently expiring.

*

Soon the young woman would know that beauty's currency was like any other: useless if hoarded, gone when spent. But as we moved deeper into winter I couldn't help noticing how your body started to resemble a snowman's — it kept melting to nothing when I tried to hold it close. Looking out the window, the man wondered aloud why some valleys fill with water and become lakes, and others remain simply valleys.

Tamar Yoseloff

Pictures of Spring

I: Shunga

The geisha parts her legs
to receive his cock,
a monstrous cryptid, swollen fist;

I cannot see her face
behind the fragile net, a strand
of hair fallen from its comb

but her sex is open wide,
complex, a darkened gorge
he will wreck.

II: Tokyo Metro / Ginza Line

The businessman next to me
balances a briefcase on his knees,
opens his *manga*:

two doe-eyed girls in gym slips,
hair in bunches, are ripped apart
by tigers.

The artist has taken pride
in the tearing of limbs,
the beauty of the tiger.

III: Isetan Department Store Shinjuku

The girl behind the counter
converts a sheet of paper
into a full blown rose:

she works quickly, her fingers
light, thin, her hair falls
across her face;

as she hands me this gift
without looking up, she nods,
a blush masking her cheeks.

IV: Ukiyo

I bend and break, bend
and break, contort my limbs
into these lovelocked shapes,

my desires spread out
like the fingered leaves
of a pillow book;

I resume the polite tedium
of clothes, desire folded in on itself –
a sharp intake of breath

Philip Terry

Stone I cut i

Of he | who see | to the | very | bottom | I will | sing ...
the wise | ~~one~~ the | man who | know all | the earth
+ + + in | ~~the old~~ | day ...
I will | tell the | story | of the | one who | know ev | ery | thing
    + + +
... DIC | TATOR | who find | the sec | ret place | open | the sec
    | ret door
and bring | back know | ledge + + + | of the | age be | fore the |
    great wave* –

                                                      *see Stone XI
he walk | the path | over | come with | pain tired | out + + +
and print | the first | stone book

He build | the wall | of big | city | of the | ani | mal noise
the wall | of the | holy | church of | the wo | man ~~sex~~ | ~~god~~ place
    | of peace
Look at | the wall | the top | be like | steel ...
Exam | ine the | in side | wall that | no hand | can match
Feel the | stone door | frame old | as the | mountain
enter | the ho | ly church | house of | the wo | man sex | god +
    + +
a work | no dic | tator | can eq | ual + + + | to this | + + + day
Climb the | wall of | big ci | ty of | the an | imal | noise + + + |
    walk on | the hard | stone + + +
exam | ine the | base in | spect the | perfect | brick work
Clock that | even | the cen | tre is | of strong | brick from | the
    fire
As for | the base | be it | not set | + + + out | by a | wise man?

One ar | ea | contain | the ci | ty one | are | a the | fruit tree |
    one ar | ea | the ~~mine~~
The three | togeth | er with | the mine | make up | big ci | ty of
    | the an | imal | noise …

Find the | metal | box full | of cut | stone + + +
slide op | en the | steel lock
open | the sec | ret door | that hold | the + + + | story
Take out | the blue | stone and | read the | book + + + | out loud

How DIC | TATOR | suffer | every | hard ship

over | power | the en | emy | the pow | er full | other –

strong one | child of | big ci | ty of | the an | imal | noise pow |
    er full | ~~man cow~~
He stand | in the | front like | a fear | less man
He march | at the | back like | a + + + | brother
a nuc | lear | weapon | to pro | tect the | army
He be | a great | wave that | break down | the wall
Son of | big ci | ty of | the an | imal | noise
DICTA | TOR be | the blue | print of | power
… DIC | TATOR | beauti | ful like | a jew | el + + +
son of | + + + WILD | COW he | mother

He op | en the | mountain | pass …
dig the | deep well | on the | mountain | side …
he tra | vel a | cross the | + + + sea | to where | the sun | god rise
travel | to the | very | edge of | the world | the one | who look |
    for the | secret | of life
he find | a way | to the | ONE WHO | FIND LIFE | the far | off
    + + +
the one | who bring | back life | when the | great wave | destroy |
    it …

+ + + fill | the land | again | with pe | ople + + +

Be there | a dic | tator | like he | in an | y land?
Who with | DICTA | TOR can | ~~profess~~ | "I am | all pow | er full!"

From he | first birth | day they | call DIC | TATOR | by this | name ...

Stone I Cut ii

Two part | god he | be one | part man
The wo | man sex | god int | erfere* (?) | with the | form of | he bo | dy ...
      *or "shape"
She add | the ~~great~~ | ......

Over | big ci | ty of | the an | imal | noise he | turn he | eye + + +
like a | wild man | cow that | stand tall | nose up | ear op | en + + +
Through the | ~~holy~~ | church he | run wild | ......
with all | the young | blade of | big ci | ty of | the an | imal | noise + + +
When he | fire he | rocket | he have | no eq | ual ...
Then the | enem | y burn | + + + + + +
he peo | ple a | wake to | battle | noise + + +

DICTA | TOR for | bid the | son to | go to | the fat | her ...
all day | and all | night + + + | you hear | the weak | cry out –
DICTA | TOR who | rule ... | over | + + + big | city | of the | ani | mal noise
Be this | ~~the one~~ | we want | to lead | us pow | er full | bright wise | in thought?
DICTA | TOR for | bid the | + + + lit | tle girl | to go | to see | the moth | er ...

the young | woman | to see | the + + + | ~~one she~~ | love the |
   woman | to see | the hus | band + + +

The ... | god hear | the cry
the + + + | sky god | ... [speak | to] the | + + + god | who pro
   | tect the | city

"Be it | you that | make this | wild pow | er full | man cow?
When he | fire he | ... rock | et he | have no | equal
Then the | enem | y burn | + + + + + +
he peo | ple a | wake to | + + + bat | tle noise
DICTA | TOR + + + | keep the | son and | the fat | her a |
   part night | and day
Be this | the man | to ~~gov~~ | ~~ern big~~ | ~~city~~ | of the | ani | mal noise?
Be this | the one | to lead | ~~the peo~~ | ~~ple~~ ...
Power | full + + + | bright wise | in thought?
DICTA | TOR + + + | forbid | the lit | tle girl | to see | the + + +
   | mother
the young | woman | to see | the + + + | ~~one she~~ | love the |
   woman | to see | the hus | band + + + "

When [the | sky god] | + + + hear | the peo | ple cry
he call | to the | GREAT MOTH | ER "You | mother | who cre |
   ate man
now make | + + + a | second | DICTA | TOR may | they be | ...
   eq | ual*(?) in | spirit |
                                      *or "opposite"
   and heart
May they | fight a | gainst each | other | so that | big ci | ty of |
   the an | imal | noise may | have qui | et ..."

When the | ~~GREAT~~ MOTH | ER hear | this she | make a | +
   + + ~~pic~~ | ~~ture~~ of | the sky | god in | she heart
Then the | GREAT MOTH | ER wash | she hand | take up | a ball |

of wet | earth and |
    throw it | in to | the wild | place + + +
In the | wild place | ... she | make WILD | MAN the | battle | fit
she | give birth | ... to |
    one like | the god | of war | in dark | and sil | ence ...

With thick | hair he | whole bo | dy be | cover
with hair | like a | woman | he head | be co | ver + + +
Like the | hair of | the wo | man corn | ... god
the lock | of he | hair grow | fast ...
He know | neither | famil | y + + + | or home | he dress | like
    the | cow god
Along | side the | wild horse | | he feed | on grass
along | side the | ~~wild an~~ | ~~imal~~ | ~~he~~ drink | + + + at | the wa |
    ter hole
along | side the | busy | ani | mal in | the wa | ter he | heart
    grow | light like | a spi | rit ...

The man | who hunt | and kill | ... an | imal | CATCATCH
see WILD | MAN ... | at the | + + + wa | ter hole
one day | – a sec | ond a | third – CAT | CATCH + + + |
see WILD | MAN | at the | water | hole + + +
when he | see WILD | MAN he | body | freeze ...
when he | see WILD | MAN he | hand freeze
when he | see WILD | MAN he | eye freeze
WILDMAN | and he | ani | mal to | gether| make the |
thing that | be not | welcome
+ + + CAT | CATCH sense | trouble | he wo | rry he | go ...
    | quiet
he heart | ~~hurt~~ + + + | he face | grow dark | under | the eye
The sad | thing en | ter he | heart ...
He face | be like | that of | a man | who tra | vel a | long road

Astrid Alben

Venus

The only machine in the sky is the sun very bright
not stare is a bottomless blue as if the clouds never existed.

Poet & I stare two-some then some blinded by specks *bzzzzzzing* in
the mesosphere like poppy seeds the cosmos blazing on your brow

I love you today Poet with your devoted crater eyes
let's love each other just the two of us

apeman spaceman
the sun asleep in our dreams where flies explode.

Betrayal

The bar in the Prince Alfred on Castelmain Street covered in blood
in Brussels there is blood on your demands for peace outside the
     chippie

stick-thin lasses in shoes covered in blood the sleazy rain covered in
blood the Spyder Porsche parked in a side street covered in blood

this morning's headlines covered in blood the awe-inspiring
symmetry of misery covered in blood and all the wasters at the bar

at lunchtime in the Prince Alfred on Castelmain Street covered in
     blood.
Hows and whens tiptoeing away *en pointe* covered in blood.

Every material

When you are finished reading can you turn off the light?
Poet lies puzzled up against your back, sleeping.

The light is out. Funny,
people disappear in cracks of the city against the skyline of

a flat field disappear in the folds of the bed between the cracks
of your fingers require a blind woman's skill like the letter S

smells of earth smells of clay of long
wires through short histories.

Portnall Road

I leave my flat a little after ten
And walk along the street
With the lackadaisical conviction
Of my semi-complicated days stowed
In a recess of the Milky Way.
I whistle a tune in E flat—
—Press on. I two-step
Past the Italian architect who thinks
Her Ethiopian child simply *duhvine*.
I wave at sweet old bygone Sue,
Her hair a-shine with Elnett Satin Extra Shine.
She's tilting on her windowsill in a pink peignoir.
It's nice to see her smile, all neoclassical bust,
All set to be jettisoned by time.
Outside the Four Faces Take-Away
Two *bruvvers* from the *endz*
Nudge their Nike LunarGlides against a trough
Of terracotta flowerpots: their disappointment
And fatigue a homegrown paradigm.

Where is their rage?
What has happened to the times?
Rebellion is as rare as caviar.
If 'history is made in the street',
As Goebbels said, it's certainly not on mine.
This street is trading up,
It's changing gear.
From tilting sweet old bygone Sue—
—New money ages overnight,
And night is drawing near.
Only the dogs,
Pent up in basement flats bark without an alibi.
I halt at the end of the street,
Whistle in E flat, relight my cigarette
(A Chesterfield) and crane my neck
At the brutality of Trellick Tower.
The windows glint like tiny fish eggs dipped in ink.
Even dinosaurs have to sleep.
They lay their fontanels to rest
On pillows provided by the Galaxy Motel.
I hear the silence tremble as they snore.

Amy Wright

Amys vs. Jennifers vs. Vonda

A slew of christened Amys inundated 1970s
grade schools named not for secretaries of state
or aunties, but a swell of post-free-love beloveds

whose generic-fearless parents chortled.
More forgettable than the average Nora,
Amys developed eclectic tastes for ecru, birch

beers ubiquitous vending machines don't stock.
Mere initials partitioned, Amys earmarked
booklists depicting little women unlike them.

The only harpsichord-playing Bottetourt
County Birdie prompted Amys' penchants
for firefighter-uniformed-Pomeranians

calendars, indigo heirloom carrots.
Even the most-popular laurel denied them,
umpteen Elizabeths crowned more common,

Amys scored thrift store faux-fur *ushankas*,
learned Punjabi, compensated
for babyish nicknames with snakeskin boots.

Still, an occasional magnate
proves standout, extricates from the hoi polloi,
dons an ankle-length peignoir regal as any Ingrid.

Gravitational forces of sameness
don't break nonpareil almond-
eyed Aberdeens less desperate to prove

a name is more or less an in
or out of circulation product, a net
three birthday party cyclists circle,

tongues swapping distinguishing
syllables which repetition obliterates
until they are all unnameable as beach glass.

Amys Orbit Golden-Ruled Pancakes

Amys who have become plural through unity
consciousness retract their parking ticket
grievances, which sets off household nitpick dominos

about Melissa's halitosis and John's brother Barnabas's
randy karaoke. Whatever department licensed
mental-glove-compartment-dumping they want silenced

without initiating a jihad against jeremiads
and assembly-not-included leftover swing-set doodads.
Would that instead they set off gratitude avalanches

for physically challenged mannequin models
in evening gowns. But no one thought of that
until Millicent regurgitated courtroom drama verbatim,

Cotton insulted his undercooked chikin' popsicle
sandwich, and Steph out-grouched the police chief,
to her detriment.

If only Amys spawned high school bless-you epidemics,
better relish-bottle etiquette, small talked more often
with their neighbours, they might throw an extra kabob

on the barbie, tyre sellers offer fourth tyres gratis,
drycleaners notice they dropped a dress size, sous chefs
compliment short-order cook's help, and servers earn

wages representative of their services rather than diners'
not-a-morning-person temperaments
and other narrow visions of human nature.

Janet Sutherland

How the dementia left some things unsaid

We could not talk of the oysters
whose workmanlike remains we'd found,
in the old field called *Horatio*;

Your plough had passed closer than usual
to a barbed wire fence and where it turned
the thin soil into chalk a cache of oyster shells

swam upwards to the light, ruffled, calcified,
lined with pearl. Whose lips had tasted
liquor salt as sea? Who buried them like coins?

Nor could we speak of roses, bruised
by a rainstorm or by winds that heaved
stem against stem until the thorns

had grappled the white sails, the blushed,
the rosy sails, the blood red broken sails
and brought them tumbling down.

In winter we would heel them in, knowing
that spring would break the leaf buds
all along the stalk. I lent you *Rosa Gallica*

when things got tough. It settled in
hard by the shore at Hengistbury Head
growing in sand, unlikely as that is.

grid ref TQ494051

Skylarks have risen in full song   the weald is blue
Too early yet for lambs the turf is short and winter
green   Distance is key   The shepherds skirt
the hills   their dog a dark brown clot that dips
and feints   always withdrawing as the flock
rips and repairs towards the field edge and a gate
We see them flowing down the lane under the skeletons
of leafless trees   Chalk, bark and fleece —the intersect
of movement in the ochre, brown and cream   Buds
are about to burst   these saplings zebra stripe the road
crowned with black buds still cold, still motionless

Smith and 9th

A girl in a daffodil dress
got on at Smith and 9th
and she was a Golden Oriole
wearing her quilted frock.

A baby's face in sepia
was printed across her breast
and her satchel strap took out the smile
across its rose bud lips.

We who may travel with her
will never know her name.
A girl in a daffodil dress rode by
shy Golden Oriole

Letters to the Evacuee

We had a bad night last night
The Goods Yard is still blazing
    I've just come in from lying
    sunbathing in the field
    to find a card from you
Jesmond Road got it, Windsor Cres.
Easlington Terrace, City Road, Shortridge Terrace
    I am so glad to hear
    you're nicely settled in
    What a job we have
They say it's pitiful in Shield Road
Children running round hunting for their mothers
    covering the windows each night
    It takes ages. We put up
    blankets and brown paper
Dolly hasn't come home but I think she's in
the feeding centre
    Last night six planes tore over
    This child peacefully slept
    through. The search lights
I got awfully worried last night, Elly and Lois
were in town but they eventually got home
    were lovely on Thursday night
    floating about in the sky
    with no beams showing
The bombs were dropping
as they arrived.

Samir Guglani

X-ray

Perfect arc of hip
a mottled half moon,
and my caught gaze widens in surprise
at your thigh's white field,
its pencilled fence of skin.
X-rays stencil broken bone,
fractured spirits,
even keep a god's bruised face.

Strange then to happen
on this living trace of human flesh, visible
but missed for years, revealed
now like a trick, like silence, loud
once the sound stops dead.

Returning

Like jostling for the first
glimpse of sea we'd listen
for my father coming home,
his signal a breath
or the pause before speech,
how I imagine his pain
was uttered that day.

Years later I spy you first,
sat reading in reflections
your mouth incanting words.
You are a coin shining
in water. I tap the window
and you stir then open
as you always do the door.

The ark

Sky drops, turns roofs to glass,
polishes them like pebbles, brings
fossils out on front paths
and returns the sea to these streets.
I cycle to you through burnt air and light,

four again—arms, oars, hooked
at a nursery window
rowing an ark
against the odds, rain and time
to this room, where waters meets us

and your chest drains fluid,
your breath a time-lapsed
tide. Legs salt swollen and trousers rolled
ready, leaking life, you look at me
all a-wink, then wade out.

Fingerprints

Look at how we start, like fortune-tellers, at the hands. Here by the window, where ward meets world, I examine this man's, turn them over like found leaves. They're remarkable, creaseless, a baby's, glass palms reflecting my own: now white, now brown. He laughs at my surprise. A tree surgeon's hands, he says, my skin pressed into other life, its bark and blood, just like you doc I bet, your fingerprints handed to others. His hand shakes in mine, shakes mine. I listen to his heart. Not scared, he says, not of this anyway; but maybe, look, of that daytime moon, the lit rock of it, what it is, what it means we are. Or those starlings, did you see this morning? Against the sky like flung dust. I think our bodies are this, that we merge really, collide and become the breath of others. Here, he says, go on, have a whiff. My fingers drum his chest. Did you hear those sounds, he asks, from that comet, like whale song, mermaids? The ship they landed, its name, what, Philae?—it means end, or place's edge, some frontier where things meet. That girl on my street told me when I dropped her a pound. She's like you, dark-skinned but sodden cold. Will you see her now on your rounds? Listen to her? It's these distances I regret—enormous, tiny—their harm. I shine a light in his ears. Hard now to tell which of us is speaking, where the voice comes from. One of us says thank you. I go to wash my hands but, seeing them in the water, stop, turn, return to him.

Home

Later, on the train home,
trees are arteriograms,

cut hearts containing
the whole winter sky.

Birds' flight is slowed,
reeled in so each wing's

discrete beat is a systole
pulsing the river's slate light.

Fields stretch and tilt, an ocean
frozen mid-swell,

the glittering flotsam
of cattle, our passing.

A Wedding Horse

'A Met Office graphic shows the path of a storm that has brought Saharan dust to the UK. It is most apparent in parts of southern England, the Midlands and East Anglia.'
                                    BBC News, 2 April 2014

You can see India from here,
its wet press of monsoon air,
then, undressing by the window, you wonder
if ghosts amount to this:
exact margins and surfaces of bodies or land
lifted and thrown place to place. Time
unclear, incipient morning or seeped dusk, just
some first spring light attaches lustre to you.
Even the streets, you say, *look,*
are decorated overnight with shrines.

Blossom stirs in a thought of rain,
a hundred bonfires glimpsed
from a rickshaw at night, faces
in the dark, a sudden white horse caught
cantering through traffic to a wedding,
lost but kept like lightning on the retina.
Surely the same one still carrying my father, in sepia,
to his bride, England, all of this—
bejewelled, in silk, eyes dressed red,
blood-lined with a bright, contained pain.

You draw close again, become breath
held at my mouth. Past you, further out,
cars recede up an erased hill,
rising slowly through the dust, like fireflies.

Helen Tookey

Rheidol Valley

> Sie war schon aufgelöst wie langes Haar
> und hingegeben wie gefallner Regen
> und ausgeteilt wie hundertfacher Vorrat
> —Rilke, 'Orpheus. Eurydike. Hermes'

If you put out your hand and the earth
were to take it, drawing you down
to its deepest bargaining-place—

If the joints of your hips had been
hollowed by water, the swallow-
holes scoured in the gorge were

your eyes, your name dissolving
like limestone in rain—

If you shook out your skirts and the earth
made grain of you, scattered and
sowed you, unmemoried, mute—

If you put out your hand and the earth
were to take it—

That Day Off Sakhalin

The anthropologist from Siberia
is singing the praises of Manchester.
—But don't you miss the snow, I ask idiotically.
We agree that Russian poets lived tragic lives.
In Soviet times, she says, there were *Houses*

for Holidays, retreats for people with talent,
scientists, artists, writers like her father.
Such people are lovely, she says, but sometimes
they need to be absent. It's not rudeness,
she says, just that sometimes they need
to be absent, exploring a thought.
Siberia? I am thinking of Zina,
that day off Sakhalin. White bay city,
blue cold water. Zina, bottle-blonde, strong
and lovely, swimming out to the yachts,
laughing at helpless naïve Slava
who will get her her ticket; out
past the buoys, strong arms, blonde hair
streaming in blue water. All through the book
they keep coming back to it, *that day
off Sakhalin*, their strange shared dream,
white bodies, pale sun, and Zina swimming,
strong and reckless, out past the yachts,
past the buoys, foreseeing her fate perhaps but
always swimming, heading out alone to some
unknown free horizon—

That Night in the Woods

So what *did* happen, that night in the woods?
    You're obsessed. I've watched you by hours, peering in through the trees, muttering to yourself. Jumping every time the car door slams, shaking your head distractedly when that fly starts buzzing. Trying to make the connections. The lights in the cabin coming on. The yelling. The glass smashing. The gunshot. The lights going out. The door. Footsteps, going away, into the trees. The telephone ringing, ringing.
    And who is it that drives up in his car, while we're in the cabin doing all the yelling? Whose heavy footsteps, right up close to you, crunching over snow—or is it leaves, dead leaves and twigs? And those small metallic sounds, something turning, locking into place—what are they?

The glass. I bet you're wondering by now just how many wine-glasses we've smashed. How many bottles, how many mirrors.

Haven't you guessed? We've got a tape loop. We set it playing when we see you coming, and we yell and we scream over the noise of it. Sometimes, I *have* smashed a real glass, just for a change. Just to see whether you would notice. Of course, you didn't. Well, you don't think we're really here. How could we be, in our tiny forest cabin, beyond a few plastic trees, all inside a clever wooden box on stilts?

Ah, but you *do* want to know, don't you, what happened that night? You do keep coming back and putting on the headphones and listening and peering through the trees, trying to make it out. So you do know, somehow, don't you? Some part of your mind is worrying away, is telling you *there's something there, something really happening...* that's why you keep coming back.

Look at you, headphones clamped to your ears, trying to see further into the dark, into our tiny windows, trying to see what isn't there. Imagining our kitchen, our living-room (is that bluish light coming from the TV?), our—oh yes—our bedroom. You're wondering what I'm wearing. What I've done to *provoke* him. You listen and listen but you can never quite make out the words, can you?

There's a reason for that. Haven't you guessed? Don't you think we'd get tired of it, the yelling, the screaming, don't you think we'd get bored?

Look. I'll show you. Here I am, relaxing on the sofa in my best satin robe, bare feet, glass of wine. The TV is on, you were right about that. He's in the kitchen, fixing us something to eat. Later, we'll go into the bedroom.

And the gunshot? The door? The footsteps? (*Is* it snow, or is it dead leaves?) The telephone ringing, ringing? What *did* happen, that night in the woods? You tell me. You tell me.

(Based on the installation *Cabin Fever*
by Janet Cardiff and George Bures Miller, 2004.)

Ian Davidson

Bridge Poem

It was an old
car anyway and
near the end of its
life but the
thing we talked
about was remi
niscent of that
other thing, you
know that thing
we never talk
about you know

It was a long
bridge anyway
across the hum-
ber or the
tyne but that's a
bridge for you
these are bridges
we can cross
on foot or behind
the wheel for
hours on end

Bridges have
to be top down
and bottom up
and the bit in
the middle
might sway
in a stiff wind an
earthquake is
undetectable in

a car on a
bridge these
are insulatory
factors, rubber
mainly, and wire

and then in
the centre of
the bridge I turn
and ask you what
do you think is
this a place to
stop and think and
look both back
and forward and
ask yourself I
like the dead
centre of a bridge
with its bouquets
of flowers

but sometimes I
just drive across
in my old car
and avoid the
lightning strikes
or the sudden
drops or the views
of the rivers down
below I always
travel across a
bridge to work
it makes my
head spin

Remember

You do remember
Don't you?
Not yesterday,
Shuffled off in a
Defragmenting disc
Drive that sleep
Won't replenish,
Bits falling away like
Your fine hair
That the wind
Easily shifts and from
The split ends narratives
That can't cohere become
Lost amongst the silver
Sand while all the while
Those structures that
Support your past have
Foundations even
Time cannot touch

I do remember
You have learnt some
Phrases that can be
Used to cover any
Situation you are
Becoming confused
But try to cover it up
And avoid the exposure
Of the telephone where
Only words will do
And no one else can
Fill in the gaps that
Like teeth that have
Been pulled too early

They are small
Triumphs the
Times you can
Pull something
Out of the bag
And for just a
Second the
Smile you always
Wore when things
Had not got quite
So blurred

Sabiyha Rasheed

Dutchman Jumbee

Dutchman Jumbee dug fingernails in soil and taste the hot earth. Dutchman Jumbee take *land of many waters* and drink until he sick. Dutchman Jumbee heave into Essequibo, the water blister and cry. Dutchman Jumbee take blue of Essequibo to push into his eye. Amerindian wash with Essequibo water and their skin become Dutchman skin. Amerindian contours mapped on trees and Dutchman say he grow it. Dutchman tree with Dutchman lung, steal Guyana air. Dutchman breath woven into silk of Guyana's heat and light. Dutchman want Amerindian hair to tie wrist and neck. Amerindian fade into Guyana soil, become paths under Dutchman feet.

Dutchman Jumbee throw rope across sea and drag Africa by the neck. Dutchman howl shatter the moon to rain on purple night skin. Dutchman Jumbee hide in Dutchman tree when blackness become blacker. Black man sing with Guyana winds to make Dutchman skin shake. Dutchman chew on black man tongue so he never sing again.

Dutchman jumbee burning leaves
Making ash of all its beauty

Carving red, gold and green into forearms
Of those who got caught in the rope

Pickney Tongue

Pickney tongue, wet and sour
Sharper than cutrass blade
Drip and spit staccato shards
To cut the coolie nigger skin
And draw faces in the blood

Coolie water rice
To Pig Tail, Brown Girl
Nigger man sala
To Black Boy, Scabby Knee

Wash your beatie with dahl and rice
Pink lip on dark boy let out laugh
That fly and sting like marabunta

Teef your mommy ten dollar
Coolie gal play jump rope
Jumping on nigger boy ribs

Mango yellow, mango green
Plantain yellow, plantain green
Still mango, still plantain
Pickney coolie, pickney nigger
Still pickney
Bleeding
Red, gold and green

Moongazer

When Moongazer stood, with his hands resting on his narrow hips, he thought of nothing but night, and what accompanied it. Thin rolls of skin would appear at the back of his neck as he tilted his head upwards to inhale the dark. He stood taller than Guyana's largest tree, back muscles flexed and legs parted. His eyes filled with moon rocks and the heat of the stars that peppered the sky. He sometimes imagined the moon as a fruit that he wished to take a bite of and watch moist flesh and moon lit liquid pour over Guyana's soil. On the nights when the sky seemed hollow, Moongazer would listen to the Moon's stories, of how he once lit the path for escape, had to hide when white hands tried to steal him from the sky and gave hope to those who only got a rare glimpse of him. The Moon's stories would make Moongazer weep until the sun emerged. His deep howls would echo for miles, causing restless nights. Moongazer became infuriated by the Moon's stories and resented humans for their cruelty. He promised the Moon he would protect him. He swore that if he were to look down and see anyone passing through his legs, walking towards the Moon, he would crush them between his calves and give their souls to the stars.

Moongazer kept his promise,
crushing bone to white powder

Letting blood feed the night
As they did in the day

Dorothy Lehane

Visuo-Motor

these are real problems— really existing—
group 5 problems (aphasic & paranoid)
in addition to organic psychoses
paralysis of musculature speech
& not receiving reliable sensory information
there's never relearning the route round the house
we are surviving one type of death
a heedless sort of narcissist death
thoughts are unitary, sentient in that moment
grant me license to dismantle all previous experience
under the trope of consummation
the linguist   made up of the radical
is post-operatively mainlining stimulus
explain proverbs
the jaw deviates to the right on excursion
the patient chokes
the patient can initiate phonation for 5 seconds
can protract and retract tongue
neglect items on the right
in the absence of the volta
you precious, cool motherfucker
95th percentile the way that sonnet begins

damned good mouth

they stop traffic with
their façon de parler
cutting across modalities
all vehicle & no tenor
nothing is as fixed as
the tongue in delirium
knocked off my feet
by claudication
by wanting normal salutations
by modular thinking
i've been putting your name
in my mouth again
in a planetary context
i'm waiting for collapse
temporally out of phase
here's to endless interlacing
of psycho-geographies
here's some dirt for your eye
& here's to the end of mating rights
stakes are high in the high teeth
& here's to the end of poledancing
to Lakme flower duet
& here's to red wine & cunnilingus
John Martyn was not faking it
i'd go as far as a Czechoslovakian box mine
or a crack den in Faversham

your stumbling/your stalled/your parataxis

i will touch you teach you   to quieten
    your-   everyday-   trauma-
    & teach the clitoris to sing-song
        we find those lovers arguing in a foreign tongue so
beautiful

                    being so far away from our own concerns :
    give up
    looking at the girls in the changing room
        if you could speak   could mourn our
lovemaking if I could love

never understanding
                        where the waist begins

 & i'd ask so many things   if I were the first born
be all be all and end all fingers in ovaries fingers in lent

skulking pheromone mother said   your skulking pheromone

                keep tally of the love-making

Ian Seed

from Identity Papers

Discovery

When my mother was told she had cancer, my father managed to sprain his ankle. He seemed resentful that she was not well enough to look after him in the way she usually did. He was in a lot of pain, he shouted, propped up on pillows in bed. My mother took to sleeping in the spare bedroom. She gazed endlessly out of the window, a small girl about to set off on a great adventure alone.

Ramblers

It was a cold dry day. We were out walking over forest-covered hills. There was a man from India with us who spoke little English, but who kept smiling. He carried an old sack over his shoulder. Like his smile, his sack made us suspicious, but we didn't ask him what was inside. When we stopped in a clearing to eat our sandwiches, he gathered some twigs and lit a fire.

While we watched, afraid yet curious, he opened the sack and brought out a pot and ladle. With just a few ingredients and water, he had soon made a spicy, sweet-smelling broth. I was the first to try it. Thus, he won his way into my heart, for it was like nothing I had ever tasted before.

Guest

Walking with my wife and daughter in the park, I came across a small boy. He started throwing stones at us. I went up to him and grabbed his wrist. 'Where do you live?' I asked as gently as I could. To my surprise, he said he would show me. He took me down a hill to a small wood. He led me to a tin hut which he shared with his mother, grandmother and older sister. They invited me in, and made me a strong black tea. I remembered I had left my wife and daughter back in the park. I wondered if they would believe my story about the family in the tin hut.

Leak

There's a beautiful girl who keeps pursuing me, but I prefer the melancholy and easy intimacy of my wife. One evening when I'm on my own at home, I hear the girl calling me from the street outside. At the same time, it starts to rain. The rain becomes so heavy, it leaks in through the ceiling. Why didn't my wife and I sort this out when we still had the money to do so? And why hasn't she come back home yet? It's almost time for me to lock everything up and go to sleep.

Offer

When I wake, we have arrived at a small, deserted station. It is already dark. An old man, who looks like a farmer, is sitting opposite me. I ask him when we will arrive at X.
　　He smiles. 'Oh, that was a long time ago. You've been asleep for hours.'
　　I wonder if I should get off while I still can and wait for a train back, even if it means spending the night in the station.
　　As if reading my thoughts, the old man says, 'There's some time yet. Why don't you join me for a drink down the road?' He gestures through the train window into the darkness in what I take to be the direction of a pub.
　　'All right, but just for one,' I say.
　　I have heard that the beer this far north is very strong. I need to keep my wits about me if I am ever going to make it home.

Being True

I kept hanging around the town, even though I had lost my job. In particular I hung around a bar frequented by literary bohemian types, among them a vampish woman who dressed Goth-style and who was having an affair with a German publisher of experimental poetry. One evening at a party she pinned me to a wall and glued her lips to mine. I had no desire to escape—I had never been so expertly kissed in my life—but out of the corner of my eye, I could see the publisher getting more and more annoyed. He stood up, called for silence and gave a small speech, in which he quoted a German proverb to illustrate that the only life worth living was the one where you were true to the thing you loved. However, his translation into English didn't quite make sense. When I extricated myself from the woman and questioned him about the translation, he challenged me to a fight. I backed away and wandered off into the night. How could I ever persuade him to publish my book of poetry now? Some kind of animal followed me down the road. Because of the dark I couldn't see what it was, but it refused to be shaken off.

Claire Crowther

Night Visiting

Stand at her door and look at her
during her aeon of sleep.
Make certain. A parent must.
What is visitable of her?

I'm afraid to move towards
a cot slowed by its creature,
who hardbuilds grit into her nest,
and not one feather nor
fascinator in her hair.

I mustn't disrupt the night thing
she does. So I will say no
to birds. Or water avens
flowering from limestone pavements
in grikes, or seeded achenes
draped with peachy sepals.

Report From The Goddess Who Handles Child Stars

The park flooded
on the last morning
she saw me.
The sash windows
creaked. The handles pushed locks.

Cold air walked up
to her bed – I was
bringing her
a different warmth.
She took my instructions –

after she'd rolled
her socks down to in-
visible –
Leave your father.
Last night's storm is our dream.

Shaking like a
primordial wave
of gravit-
ation, she left
home. Roots loosened. The streams

in Jubilee
Park where floodwater
toes channels
dug by humans,
exploded. Last years' annuals

offered dead sticks.
Beyond the barn's broken
spine, crow-nest
ferns parted, let
her through. *Leave the green bug*

in its spit. Where
nettle bows to you,
a boy waits.
In her country
hurt canes the dirt with rain.

Keith's Watch

As often as a boy spits on the pavement
in front of me

Keith sets his watch at bedtime. You think time leaks
breath? No, it clogs

inside lungs. It needs to be hawked. It needs clocks.
I'm confident,

not sidestepping
spit, Keith will make sure we wake up together.

David Miller

Spiritual Letters (Series 7, #3)

As we stood at the gate, looking towards the distant bay, we suddenly heard a stonechat calling. – If we're going to their place for dinner, we need to take our own plates, not to mention knives and forks. A rustle, not of wings but of paper. Burned black. A chair, standing by itself in the room: spectral, abandoned.

> *no end*
> *or beginning*
> *to humility*
> *its foundation*
> *its increase*
> *in the central*
> *nothing*
>
> – – –
>
> islands
> mountains
> no end
> of islands
> or mountains

With violence he began to persecute and to defame for heresy the women he had known and had at one time cherished and commended as holy. We had not long set sail for the island, when a ship caught us up and came alongside, bearing word that we were to be exiled to an even more remote place. And so we changed course....

> bell tolling
> *most simple*
> *most one*

clear light
or darkness
how cold here
where? remembering
and to dream
first one book
then so many

Jaime Robles

from The Wittgenstein Vector

Proposition 2.0251
Space, time and colour (colouredness) are forms of objects.

Here.

                There.

Hearing your voice,
which keeps coming back to me,
threaded with color. We are reading
the same lines of the same poem.

You seated under unvarying light.
Me, in darkness, held still in repetitions,
remembered, so that with every
sound you exhale, my nerves chime.

•

Proposition 4.016
In order to understand the essence of the proposition, consider hieroglyphic writing, which pictures the facts it describes. And from it came the alphabet without the essence of the representation being lost.

I draw a circle around a name.
It flutters like a bird: caged though
it no longer scores the sky
with flight. Birds fall in clusters
like rain.

I draw a circle
across the sky, name its essential
color as blue. Blue, a circle inscribed
drops out of the sky. It is written
with wings
and the color of flight.

•

Proposition 4.22

The elementary proposition consists of names. It is a connexion, a concatenation, of names.

Surfaces of a stone can be smooth. Glass-like
and also markable: the chisel, like a diamond,
leaves a name, a fact, an object, a proposition,
on the clear surface, molecules are rearranged.

A name, a simple word, a fact, an object assumes
what lies beyond the window's transparency: the garden
where roses struggle to bloom under winter's
false sun, the branch of the young oak
bent under the weight of rain, its slow coursing
sap preventing the snap of broken wood.

There are birds, blades of grass and stray cats.
The brick wall of the church and the neighbor's fence.
All of these gather in the cartouche surrounding
these scratched letters, upholding logical confusions.
On a stone, as on glass, essential gardens lie below
the carved word, banging tambourines and clattering
castanets, seething across pharaonic ruins.

•

Proposition 5.153

A proposition is in itself neither probable nor improbable. An event occurs or does not occur, there is no middle course.

There are two points, drawn with chalk.
They are more than one dimension:
A thumb presses white into asphalt gray, the print
is a trail, marking events. And desire.

A line runs between them: it is two dimensions
but it is not short: it meanders, shivers in time.
Watching eyes shutter shut: the sun contracts
into pupils, black uncovering blue irises.

A radiation of lilies scatters across the ground,
scented and impossible. The improbable fans out,
is candescent. Tongues lick the sky, sizzle
with words and words: Stay! they say. Stay.

Juana Adcock

The Science of Perambulation

1. Orisson, horizon at the edge of the valley

The first thing you notice is pain, of course.
Aching thighs, coxis turning slightly. Pain
au chocolat. Tiny muscles in your bare feet
elasticate against angular gravel
brought from elsewhere.
Looking down at the sea clouds
frothing between the peaks.
The act of balancing
what was brought against
what others have.
The house hangs from your shoulders,
the washing line from the strings of your sunhat.
The stones roll from your toes up to your hip socket,
clicking.
How to walk until you've used up the last grain.
How to sleep, small, alone,
watching the tail of the Milky Way turn
on the earth's axis—a staff of almond wood,
its bark smooth in your hand.

2. Roncesvalles, valley of prickly shrubs

The Song of Roland was all about horses,
about drops of Saracen blood hanging from thorns,
and oliphants singing heroes where only death –

I drink from Roland's fountain and watch
the water get stuck between words,
oui le chanson meaning nos vamos

pa'l otro lado

how the Erdara letters were carried in gourds and wineskins
in the bellies of lutes and the jugulars of juglars
through txabolas and akelarres

over mesetas, valles y campos
finite earth

3. Irotz, the other iron-clad

Between the oven of Irotz and the mount of Nerval
there is a swarm of straw-coloured locusts.

They fly bloodwinged around your shins,
bump into your blessed pilgrim toes.

You crouch through the dusty stridulation,
knees creaking, hips clicking like locust.

I want to untie your sandals,
wash your feet in my tears like a mystic.

You know there is abundance
in having nothing.

4. Ciraqui, the circus of surplus

A monument of haystacks
red-struck by dawn. Castle-like.

And a cohort of knackered sunflowers,
bowing their heads for our sins.

How I wished to be alone.
How I left behind a man

dragging his suitcase.

5. Alto del perdón

The hill of forgiveness isn't much.
It's more the round stones, coming down,
castigating knees. Little olive trees,
giving and giving. The metallic growl
of industry, eating away at the land.
The packs of humans, descending en masse.

Pretty leaves, I wish I could keep you.

6. Grajera, grains of higher

SW W NW, floats the compass before my eyes.
A snail, translucent in the morning sun
slops that slowness is the quick of the ambulator.

A sprig of lavender in my hair, and how we woke
by the lake, on cracked mud, phosphorescent blue
mould, like the sceptre of that blue

flower of thorns. But that's not
what I wanted. I always knew what I wanted
until

until

My legs, spread out in front of me –
I rub medicinal oils in preparation
for a day's work.

How did I never know?

7. Burgos, land of burials

I ride my stone horse to the cathedral –
those stone carvings pointing up to the sky.
Like the cemetery cypress

sending sick souls up. My hips closed,
flirting with the fall. Tall windows,
to watch the red rooftops,

the windmills flying away.

8. Meseta, table plain

¿Caminante no hay camino?
Worst lie in poetry.

The path is well marked
in yellow arrows of urine.

Toilet paper strewn around edges
in case you weren't sure.

Lest you stray

Helen Moore

Migrant Neighbours

They occupy airspace round our tall Victorian houses,
wheeling, calling in a shrill, mysterious tongue, a ruckus born up
by hot winds from Africa, stirring with quixotic behaviour.

Out walking I met a brown-skinned man in a striped polo-
shirt pointing at a tree. "Look, wood pigeon nest inside!"
Peering through a screen of foliage, I glimpsed it

and thanked him for sharing the secret. "Bird don't trust
foreigner!" he replied, waving his camera.
O, white, small-town England…

sickle-shaped, mercurial, my migrant neighbours
were once called 'Devil birds'. Like scimitars
slicing through fixed trajectories –

human lives invested in bricks, mortgages ('pledges of death'),
soulless work for cruise-line retirement – Swifts are harbingers
of repressed dimensions.

Icarus, have we not learnt? Literalising the spirit's flight,
every summer crowds amass in thrall to the Red Arrows –
white male egos spewing patriotic vapour

to suck more youth into the wide-mouthed war machine.
Whistling in our dreams, Swifts soar to 10,000 feet and sleep
on the wing. Daily they return to press us –

theirs no choreographed routine, but ceaseless
improvisations with each other, with wind currents, insects;
I listen, try to interpret.

The Big 'C'

1. Three Oncologists
After the painting by Ken Currie, Scottish National Gallery

In Playfair's gallery, a broad canvas sucks the eye
into its portal (curtained in deepest hues of contusion),
where three archpresbyters of flesh take centre stage.

Even those who glance away already feel the scene
branded on their psyche, sense it haunting
dreams, spinning lonely paranoias.

Dare to watch! These allopathic men
squint back, observe our recoil from their ghoulish aura,
forms lit as if by marsh gas.

Ashen-faced, in blue and green scrubs,
fresh blood on their gloves, they'll admit
whomsoever will enter this theatre,

surrendered to the mind's reductive glimmer.
(Here's no mystery of the soul – scripts hold disease
to be the clockwork's malfunction.)

Sleight of hand, and an anaesthetist brings the body
down... like Theseus minus Ariadne's counsel...
into the labyrinth, where it lies

supine on the sterile altar, and surgeons flourish silver
instruments, make their paramedian incisions
through skin and subcutaneous fat.

Within lies the metastatic lump, which they debulk,
scraping malignant tissue with a small curette.
Little is known of Patient X –

what makes her tick.
Steady as we go! The surgeons work to fix her up, plying
their neat sutures. All being well, X will be cured,

live a long life on remission,
never to return
to that inhospitable terrain.

2. Pink Ribbons
After the film by Léa Pool

Waiting in the wings
an industry rallying women
to combat breast cancer
with pink – buying it
in specially branded things:
{trinkets, ear muffs,
furry dice, a range of car
accessories, key rings} –
armies of pink women:
victims, survivors,
friends and supporters,
all doing their bit,
jogging round Westminster
by night (while more MPs
than usual are sleeping),
raising a small fortune
for big pharma's 'Cure'
that's always on the brink
of being found,
and meanwhile enjoys
presumed success
by dyeing the world pink.

3. Outing the Mafia

Behind the scenes 'The Big C''s executive producers –
the boys alluded to, but rarely ever named.

First-off, Nuclear Radiation is sinister and invisible,
likes to infiltrate his prey, brooding,

often waiting years to strike. His brother,
Air Pollution, specialised in spewing

particulates and dioxins, is similarly imperceptible
except on hot days in cities,

when with shimmering hands he chokes his victims.
The cousin, Agro Chemical, sporting skull

and crossbones, is quite different – a garrulous type
who sprays pesticides as he peddles GMOs, insisting

the world would starve if it weren't for him.
Then there's slick godfather, Mr Postmodern Living,

on his arm an ironic supermarket basket
of products that stir up *Bloody Toxic* (body

as cocktail shaker), ingredients: nail polish, air fresheners,
tinned food, sunscreen, fizzy drinks, dry-cleaned suits,

processed meat, underarm deodorants – this inside-job
quietly conspiring to damage DNA, disrupt hormones, inflame

tissues, switch genes on or off. Meanwhile, the trouble
and strife, Mrs. Suppressed Emotion, keeps calm,

carries on running to meet hubby's every need. Such good
fellas, with multiple politicians, lobbyists and admen

in their pockets, these mafiosi are brilliantly adept
at spreading tumours, at not playing fair.

Gerrie Fellows

Watershed

i
Intent on our destination
hard core under boot soles
the track a drum

we are fenced   from lightness
of birch leaves,   sinuous pine
fenced from water
under hill names scooped with snow

bird calls cross the wire we walk between
high strung instrument
the flickering wren has no part of
nor the pine marten
doling dark scats in indented dust

(racing spokes past us at our walking pace)
we come down at last to the loch
find ourselves
         without access
to the once-were-grazings
zoned from human intervention
by human intent

ii
zoned from grazing deer:
fenced saplings   and pines
older than we can imagine
in our embodied counting
(at the pace of racers   simple walkers
in our one-time lifetime)

grandmother pine
going under   in slow motion
home to insect and lichen
nutrient to nutrient soil
how strange to us

serpentine,   cracked beauty

iii
as if we could live otherwise
in our ever-moving at evening
deeper   into the moine
against the flow
of the long east-flowing river
against ice
against the scour of glacial trough
into the catchment

the rocks of the moine slide us
over buried levels
(now we're in deep time   and counting)
hitch us also a little sinister, infinitesimally
          shift
the precipitous breached ridges

iv
We flit past the pace of geology
or ice   thinking them stilled
          to where even a river

in a space of grass and moss
is an almost imperceptible welling

before moment
          to momentum
                    /falling
                         headlong

```
                        we are
held
in gravity's tip
over the slowest transformations
of rock    over/
metasediments,    unimaginable
over
        into
                        into
```

The Life of the Field

The place where you step over
the place where your daughter holds you
    I half imagine: the field
with its creek, the big trees, some of them fallen
a branch our daughters once sprung on together

Back from the house a distant train
crosses the rough horizon of a ground
I can't, as you can, bring to mind in its detail
    grasses   tree bark   leaf mould
the clean stench of mud at the burn

        only the field   the idea of the field
        like a green skin   earth tissue
        and you finding your way through it
        in long grass   finding yourself

at the place where you used to jump
where now your foot won't work
Your body needled with information
won't give you that knowledge of landing
Your daughter finds you a stick, gives you her hand

        you step over   into the life of the field

Aidan Semmens

Stories About the Wind

and illuminates the world
gleam entering the body
the smell of its substance
plane blacked out
in spurious protection
flying blind into the glow
flash dancing in the bone

then when the shock wave hits
pummeled up another 200 feet
aircraft of such tonnage
acting like a leaf
on a blowy night
thermal curtains flying
big eyes unclosed
earth heaving and popping
old paint under a blowtorch

and a small private army
bought secondhand
stacking used engines
batteries and fuselage
wings torn off by sordid boys

we sort the plastic from each other
bundle unread newsprint
warheads past their use-by date
spent fuel rods and radiant cones
measureless buried in closely
where they will or will not
go off or leach half-lives
into a soil washed by wavelets
on unforbidden shore

and the poets of the old nations
told stories about the wind
and the planes come sparking
out of the mountains

and she paces the floor
and wants to teach fear
a sudden windshift
rumours associated with
bureaucratic detail
the bedding the canned food
lighting of the morgue
drawings pinned by the blackboard
in a schoolroom entered
by metal ladder
beneath a concrete cover in a shaft

From the Aesthetics Bureau

how did it come to this?
strange things happen in markets
the adverbs & adjectives accumulate
& walls have a structuring effect

the first business of philosophy is to account
for things as they are
the art of war & revolution
when the rhythm is quickening

a group of boys playing in Madrid
children clambering around rubble
the look of crowds in India & Russia
the furtive glee of a man on the run

what exactly is a decisive moment?
these dark tints are really in the picture

low-resolution messages to be glanced at
small gestures of humanity in the street

photos of beautiful women from behind
wrecked lives & ghostly rooms
the quality of emotion in the subject
a geometry constructed of what's offered

picturesque prostitutes & dusty people
a portrait of a woman sobbing
in the remains of a building
children crying in a crowd in rags

what can we reason but from what we know?
cities breed disease & unnatural eating
we may not look but with extreme emotion
infer the future from data about the past

images recur
there is no meaning but something
like a dream of meaning
a kiss like a gunshot or a psychiatrist's couch

how bountiful is the earth and who
holds the rights to nature's goods?
the enormous agricultural capacity
of the world's unexploited land

there will be growing revulsion against the cult
a badly crafted lie
escalating tensions & a steady rise in casualties
the dynamic of conflict itself

darkskinned boys frolic naked on the cracked earth
while girls with plaits sell fruit
logistical support from the security services
a complex reality on the ground

painting was agitation
lancing an abscess in his psyche
dark erotic optimism
a sensation delivery system

the rustle of language
the shudder of meaning
photographic accidents & faults
troops still massing near the border

dried leaves on your table catching fire
as they pass under your fingers
knots & flutters in an empty field
the dreadful irresistible life of apples

malignancy under the microscope
jags of energy & absurdity
inconvenience mud & flies
the exacerbation of colour

Lucy Sheerman

The Night Transcripts: Letters to Jane

Dearest

Her dress, a shadow of white on smoky skin. I can see the tremor of her heart. Tobacco flower blooming in a twilight garden. The sultry air like hot breath. Undone. Flames beneath the skin, burning my fingertips. Fires that glow in the darkness all through the night. I long to be done with it.

Rochester

Dearest Jane

How can I describe that look, captivating me with its disdain. I was humbled. Held still by the dead weight of need. Overpowered. I wanted to shadow my fingers across her skin and see her turn to scorn me. I wanted to ask for mercy and then I wanted her to deny it. I felt that I was heartsick and had been for a long time and that I could be cured with that scourging. It was utter. I craved pain that would show me the limits of myself. Contain me. I felt all my waiting and my wanting twisted into an ache of undesire. I had glimpsed myself reflected back; vile and disgraced. Seeking to be enthralled I sought her. But the look was gone. I was merely locked in the impulse of staring into emptiness, caught in a trap all of my own making.

Your loving,

Edward

J.E.

That hunger that rises in the heart, so strong the morning we left the island. My arms unfilled. I was free to breathe in the bitter air, felt it flowing through my veins like emptiness. A fever I'd been gripped by again and again. Despite surviving all those bouts I could never shake it off and here was the old sickness taking hold.

I longed for new faces, liberty from familiar scenes and knowing eyes. I might be anywhere. I was cut free of it all. But that old canker, lust, followed me still. And my rotten heart I carried with me too. Dark as that lock of hair I returned a lifetime ago.

Faithfully yours

E.F.R.

Dearest

Ice child. Phantom, shape shifter, sister, fairy, spirit, elf, changeling. Nestled in the shadows. I too have felt this desolation of being parted. Long loneliness. Without light, without heat. Let us summon mother or father, no sooner alive than lost. I will rock you in my own arms. Stroke your blank cheek. Who better to protect us? We could bring each other fortune. Consider, should I not have a lover, a heartsease, consoler to cradle me through these tempests? Rich torments. Do not weep. Strange child. Stranger's child. I would take you in. Give you comfort. If I were not always otherwise; flesh eating ghoul, blood sucker, crawling animal, foul corpse. Ashes and lust. Tell me of that burning love you would hold up against the fires in my heart. Warm yourself again.

Your dearest,

B

Dearest Jane

Paleness and darkness. You and I. Lips raw. Sharp kisses. I was held. Skin chafed. The red of hurt. Thin skin exposing me to feeling. Light is sudden and sharp.

Coiling, limb tangling, tongue-tying heaviness. Words all rough. Hoarse consonants. Coarse. I am thick with longing for you. Shape this roughness. Unlock my fineness. Unremember my blunt whispers.

I shadowed you through the dark garden. Longed to be outside. Saw you hold your hand across the light to him. Glittering drops shimmering with absent sun.

Your loving

Bertha

Dear Miss Eyre

I am trying to write neatly. This is not my hand. Mine is too wild, too full of loops and swirls, lists too much to the edge of the page, has full stops that are too forceful, too definite, puncturing the page. And the sentences I can never learn to hold in check – my pen scratching at – Nothing! Shall I write only the words I want to hear? Want you to hear. Want you here. Forgive me, it is impossible

Lucy Hamilton

from The Diarists

Crocodiles & Frigate Birds

It's years since the Diarist last saw it. Men had to manoeuvre it *[one good tree & axe for hollowing]* through trap-doors up to the third floor, winch it up on ceiling-rollers in two, or was it three, pieces? It's the only object of his on display in the museum *[long planks from single tree]*, one small notice with his name and the year of the Expedition. No items of clothing *[pieces of rattan]*, no diaries or sophisticated instruments. When they were small her awestruck children fingered the intricate crocodile *[carved beast for figurehead]* and the frigate birds in perpetual flight. Now the canoe is suspended so high you can't see inside *[wooden weights, hooks, scrapers, thwarts, brackets]*. Last night they all crowded round, skyping a granddaughter in Bolivia. And she could see her face and hear her voice. It's amazing what that little 'periscope' can do.

Notes & Quotes

The Diarist's son owns a fibreglass sports kayak. When he goes. When he goes white-water kayaking in the Atlas Mountains. Only a Greenlandic kayak is called *qajaq*. C's kayak would be *qajariaq* meaning 'like a *qajaq*'. Each man's qajaq is built to the specifications of his own body. *I always tried to make it so that it was not too short – so that I could load the insides with skins and provisions.* The Inuit copy the animals – that ivory bear Uncle Tom sent for her 10th birthday! – match the skins to parts of their own body. The women stitch a seal-gut jacket – *tuilik* – with bone-needle. Sew two-layered leather stitching not to hole the fabric. To retain water-tightness. To stiffen where necessary. C. wears his neoprene wetsuit & jacket. When he goes whitewater kayaking on the Oued

Ouzoud. When he wears his fibre-glass crash-helmet. When he plunges between rockfaces. Flies between water & sky.

Bedtime Stories

I

And the Diarist smiles, seeing as vividly as yesterday their eager little faces pleading to hear again & again: *In the worst and deepest of the rapids, we touched a sunken tree, upset, and the canoe went careering bottom up down the stream.* The father she hardly knew ... *I got caught in some of the underwater branches of the tree, was dragged deep down to where it was horrible and quite dark* ... How still they lay and rapt, eyes wide as owls'. Oh, the times he escaped by a feather! *I was carried along by the current at a hideous pace towards another swift and deep rapid ... which would certainly have been the end of me, had the Dyak not caught sight...*

II

Not a day goes by that she doesn't think of Mother. Mother who was 'waiting until you were old enough to understand'. Standing at the fireplace, turning her face away to tell what N. already knew – but he hadn't believed the boy at school. Now it was true. He would never forgive. Not until he'd eventually write the book ... *Ironically Dr. S. became better known for his appalling death than for his distinguished life.* Mother descending the stairs crying ... *For us she published a selection of his letters & diaries.* Now it's the grandchildren reading *The canoe was recovered, but the sack containing my bedding and everything else was lost.*

Mark Dickinson

Scalby Beck

Uncertainty crisp along the uncertain shore;
nowhere else but here, pinning anxiety, its
tender out of reach that blinks through the
dim uncertain hour, troubled by moods,
that sway among the latticing branches,
uninventing, pleading nonetheless the
dedication, its faint impression, a making
out from the thinning apparition of light, its
curving undersides, priming arrears, only
the soft vanishing into the vertical striations
that give across this mythic stand, its faint
wandering between the un-exacting tones.

Welcome is, since how we give or open—
gone—without conceit, distancing, the
trouble stirring as what afflicts the torrent,
or notes—this beckoning faintness, its
apparition mute.

Held so, close to, now, how going must,
beyond its comfort hold, pleading the day
out, thrashing strain, it's a terrifying echo
sowing the damage of love, neglected and
undoing the years.

Hopeful yet, in doubtful resurrection, its
ebbing streams a company in clear
transparent clouds—how it may—no! The
crippling moment of eye lust, its transcript
of geometric edge, refining the undisclosed
in-private browsing.

Holding it back, a corner faint with ready
nettle; popping balsam swaying its
multiples.

Where is the heave of benediction? Kindly
approach, its unmake carelessness, the
heavy transport of a glorious **FAIL**, how
unkindly the spoil so invested in hymn.

Help shy the faltering fox, that un-did
benefactor of a needed wisp, this way
parted the sunlit columns, clouds clear sill
before a shimmer, how it migrates entire,
probing occlusions.

This thin bare path for the deer, is fit beside
fern, its runs between fox and rabbit, may
harbour the badger.

Bait against the restless will, our terrible
blow from the social underside, tempering
the rarity of meet, that part in tears, the
hurt that I have done, met.

Sorry in truth the spores, the hinged less
flow, its liquid migraine informs the sea of
its common wends.

The knotting cleaved, the cork-screw hazel
nets the canopy to its lasting. The hour fell.

Faintly pray unwedded from a certain
origin, or knot, at all, as those, in pagan glint
through sheer of muslin pass, un-orthodox,
stoned—where the gritty pilgrim sounds a
hint of linnet, which strays into another
moment's rapid constellation.

How greets the great crested threshold hurled across?

Pining stippled gauze that traces half a whisper to those tiny mythic wings.

Held again in the calm duration of what's passed between the ways not gone.

Fledge or flushed—the jagged strung its mottled ravine; the steadying glide imparts the wash, its' shone on stony threshold sways across the radials.

Ravishing culverts upon a meek—weirwhite darkening; how we sought our own displeasing; though gristles of light upon a nib, fall on a soft track sticky with footfalls, idly passing through sheaves of grass.

Its glint, a freshness fleshing the bustles of the many common dazzles, among miniature dancing heads of stars thick with scent filling the air with a heavy measure of time.

Small lingering details fade, eventually, where heady moods darken into distant cloud-sores. Break open to, our slack despondent droop. Wind forth its pith, the weight of an others memory.

Recalling, how, by turns, in the straying need have well. By darks slippage of water fall, happily held in burrs, the tenderness of his seed in you.

Before me the many fascinations, turning
over stone; Cray among sedge, stony
nymph, neither high nor naked, but
awaiting its own outcome, far from me.

We are necessarily grating the spirit road,
through dilated spectres of misuse, among
vertical corridors of abuse; our glade
dalliance sort balance among attention.

I glades gleaning aperture, porous under
skin seeping liberty through lean
escarpments, its sequential permanence
open to interjections on behalf of an
opening explicit with trammel.

Earth-sore wash-off grief where roots
tend her as guardians of slip to hold the
curve of your sea-cut.

Gripping the sore, in softly seeding
sediment, its own offer of promise lays its
detail on another shore, far-forward of
submersion.

Dark falls through air, grief, struck-toward
scar let's ragged cloys in.

Petals there laved with alternating dash,
stretched into darkness distorting space,
between spaces taken between floods
scattering the drowned.

Contemplating the anxious with grace;
structures to the flood, turning the thought
toward a leaflets willow between a catkins
slender gender dense with hair, annotated
around the points of recognition.

Trying to intern the schemes of the masters;
the attraction of capital, those soft catkins
within thicker margins read against the glut
of injury ripping through the shadow, where

Errors bid labour dreaming the dark
bleeding through skirmishing vowels.

Weir-white weld: lips of its motion going
where everything which arrives is going
gnawed along the seasons gone.

Through long swept corridors leaning
between the ontological matter and a heap
of saying—swirling with ruffles of
departure.

Hanging across the stains of attachment, its
vertical note, splicing the content of
deformity, extorting the spilling correction
that will make me care, but caring precisely

Less; it sinks into the eye of nothing,
granular enough, but indecisive at the
forceful intervals/ so parts into a distant
sea/ of irregularity.

ELŻBIETA WÓJCIK-LEESE

let us say: the house

this chosen

                minimally maintained
                by aridity and cold

immobile for days

              not a wind moves
      and the air is still inside
              the house
   holding its breath
              from the most withheld tense
              to the most relaxed entropy

soundless

            if one hears voices
            one is hearing voices
                    children's and adult voices
                          from the past
essence of abandoned abandonment

            there is nevertheless
              an oozing

            between midnight sun and midday darkness
            between tension and relaxation
            between two kinds of spirit(s)   (breath)

                time at work
            slowly and suddenly retained
   and released

stretching from the edge of an image across a little polar plain to the house

        and back again

                        across the abandonment itself
        set in motion
        by a pretended movement

a feint: the image lays its membrane across its motif

Note:
An erasure of 'led os sige: huset' by Erik Gant, art critic and brother of Pia Arke, Greenlandic-Danish visual artist—Arke used his text for annotating the white frames of *Imaginary Homelands* alias *Ultima Thule* alias *Dundas the Old Thule* (1992/2003), her four silver/gelatine prints that present her childhood home in Dundas, Thule (Greenland).

Antonyms to Ignorance and Neglect 1-10
after Pia Arke's 'Nature Morte alias Perlustrations 1-10'

Perlustrations
1   audit the wheeze of an incessant wind in Scoresby Sund
2   check volume, or volumes, of Arctic soundbites
3   cross-examine how carpenter's ruler unfolds: the wooden rigidity of hindsight
4   diagnose all the mute drawers of misplaced archives
5   experiment with the prolonged blur of camera obscura – let your body lurk in its darkroom
6   explore grainy panoramas of childhoods not quite yours
7   inquire into local customs of forgetting
8   inspect the sinews of your arm stretching to reach
9   interrogate your lichened tongue, not memory
10 investigate patient reroutings of quick-silvered ripples

alias *Nature Morte*

1. observe your thumb touching your index finger, your right hand's tender bight
2. probe the moulting undercoat of a gift toy, your dog-eared past: Ittoqqortoormiit
3. question how limpets stud the white spines of Greenlandic annals
4. raid the hexagon of your face, anchored by frail collarbones in liquid dark
5. research the darned skin around the right armpit – will the heart emerge through the threads?
6. review the gilded mistrust of Danish missionaries, trapped in black leather
7. scan for shoulder drop, the painful asymmetry of the missing breast
8. scrutinise the etched rings of healing: will the life dance resume?
9. search for a matchbox to scale the mounting cinders of old ethnographies
10. study the pale promontory of your left arm, its osar of interrogation

Note:
Pia Arke's *Nature Morte* is a sequence of 10 prints (silver/gelatine on barite paper): 8 photographs, shot in the Danish Naval Library, portray Arke's hands, early missionaries' books on Greenland, an illustration of a Greenlandic healing ritual; 2 photographs, taken in a breast cancer clinic, show Arke's friend, Susanne Mortensen, poet and expert on Inuit culture.

Marina Tsvetaeva
translated by Angela Livingstone

To pass by...

But maybe the best victory
over time and over gravity
is to pass by without leaving a trace,
to pass by, not leaving a shadow

on walls...
             maybe: win by refusing?
Erase oneself from all the mirrors?
Thus – like Lérmontov in the Caucasus –
steal past, not disturbing the rocks.

Or maybe the best fun would be
not to touch with Bach's finger
echoes of organ music? Just
fall to pieces, leaving no dust

for an urn...
              maybe – win by deluding?
– Remove oneself from all latitudes?
Thus – to steal through time as through an
ocean, not disturbing the water...

1923

Night

Hour of the uncovering of the heights,
when you look into souls as into eyes.
Wide open – the floodgates of the blood!
Wide open – the floodgates of the night!

Blood was pouring. – And the pouring blood
was like the pouring night, and the night poured
like pouring blood! – The hour of hearing's heights,
when world enters ears like entering eyes.

Torn-off – the veil of visibility!
A gaping lull of time! This is the hour
when – parting our ear like lifting up an eyelid –
we neither weigh nor breathe: we only hear.

The world turns out to be all auricle,
a shell that sucks all sounds into itself.
World has become sheer soul! (This is the hour
of entering souls like entering an embrace!)

1923

Garden

After this hell,
after this rage,
send me a garden
for my old age.

For my old-age years,
calamitous years,
hard-working years,
hunched-back years.

To destitute age –
a treasure trove.
To feverish age –
a garden, cool.

A garden give
to this fugitive,
with no one at all!
not a single soul!

Garden with never
a footfall or eyeball!
Garden with never
a giggle or whistle !

A garden send
with not a single ear,
nor a single smell!
nor a single soul!

And say: "Enough of suffering. Now
for a garden lonely as herself".
(And even you, don't stand around!)
A garden lonely as I myself.

Send such a garden for when I'm old…
An 'other' garden? The 'other world'?
Send it to me for when I am old,
for the absolution of my soul.

1934

Philippe Jaccottet

translated by Ian Brinton

A Game of Patience

In the playing-cards laid down in lamplight,
fickle figures placed in dust across the baize,
through smoke I gaze at what is best
not seen on this surface.
A clink of glasses heralds more insomnia:
a rising fear of tightening time,
a using –up of life and dwindling of motive.
An old man sheds past pictures,
stifles memory and stares at hailstones
rattling on the garden gate.

Gypsies

There is a fire glinting beneath those trees;
I can hear low voices muttering
near the gates of the town:
speaking words to a world that sleeps.

If we pass with hushed steps, fleeting travellers,
between these two worlds, it is for fear
of disturbing ongoing murmurs heard
around that hidden light.

Winétt de Rokha

translated by J. Mark Smith

Sonnet to be placed along the banks of a photo album

My countenance and her attitude of honeysuckle
take indigo form
as the dust jacket upon a nest of memories.

Everything has been going dark:
the heroic gust,
the ensanguined butterfly, dancing here
and there in the sunlight.

Have you heard how the raven planted his seeds of night
and surrounded the isolated thorn tree?

All those kisses, to make reason submit;
all those roses, sentenced to the murderous triangle of pain.

Lonely, your love does nothing but spin,
like a propeller
in the light-filled garden
of a star that's nodded off...

Our Father

Often solitude
prowls around in me
to the deep hum of silence.

The obscure souls of bats
lash their dismal hopes against the windows.

Sensitive to the cold, the chimneys
roll their sad vapours
across roads liberated of all trace
of heaven and of time.

The redolence of cassie flower
keeps away evil spirits,
while I'm hammering at the glare
in the black architecture of the books.

My lamp,
like a tragedian's blade,
cuts through the heart of the dawn.

A bee hive

snugs inside my belly, ripe as fruit,
palpitating, going golden like a corn field in season —
and nothing disturbs it but *being*.

The wind agitates it, like the trembling of aspens;
beloved songs make it drowsy
when the leaves fall, as if tears
were falling but no one was crying:

it senses the kid-like steps of the goats at daybreak;
the return of the sunflowers of the afternoon;
the Southern Cross, affixed to the
naked absolute of night.

Later, it sleeps like a bamboo leaf,
tilted downward,
extending itself, like a pendulum,
without arms,
without eyes,
without voice,
matter in shade, curled up
in the red coronal of my womb.

Braids of Smoke

Because storm clouds descend
hotheaded upon the solitude of dawn
and high roofs inject a venom of boredom
and both overpower
the closed and shallow wave-forms of the day —

those butterflies, so yellow,
have come from somewhere.
They strip the petals from an ebony necklace,
my throat
an iris between two areas of nothing.

There: voiceless lambs
sacrificed on the border of morning,
there: liberated volcanoes, ruminations,
golden-haired snails kissing the mouths
of juicy little bellflowers.

The dance, all immediacy, of a wind that stinks of death—
it squats now at my feet
rubs its temples with a dropped bit of gauze.

Those laughing eyes are clear
as the days of Pentecostal fire.

My heart tosses itself
over the edge of the spaces without measure,
spiraling downward,
made real, with a handful of opals,
as if everything, absolutely everything,
were coming to pass:
I am in the hinterlands of ordinary meaning,
cagey like the rocks and stones
wondering how
(without anyone hearing them think)
they wash their faces
in the unalterability of time —

my own being drawn fine as a leaf of platinum.

Osip Mandelstam

translated by Alistair Noon

Tristia

I've studied the science of separation
at wakes when hair's worn simply.
Oxen chewing, the mourners waiting,
it's the watch's final hour in the city.
I keep the rites of the cockerel night,
as they raise the road's bitter burden,
gaze out into the distance, red-eyed,
where sobs and songs can be heard.

Who hears that word "separation"
and knows the goodbye we'll adopt,
the promise in cockerel's exclamations,
when fires will burn on the Acropolis,
and on some kind of new life's brink,
while oxen chomp under tarpaulins,
why the cockerel beats its wings,
announcing dawn on the city walls.

The shuttle warps, the spindle hums:
I love the common, humdrum threads.
Watch barefoot Delia, here she comes
toward us, aloft, like a swan's feather.
Our life unsteady on its feet,
how scanty are the tongue's delights.
We've seen it all, it all repeats,
it's the instant we taste and recognize.

Well, so be it: a glassy figure
lies on a clean, earthenware plate,
like a squirrel's spread-out skin –
bent over the wax, a girl gazes.
It's not for us to guess Greek hell.

Women have wax, bronze is for men.
The only time our lots will fall
is war, but they divine their own end.

1918

Light Rain in Moscow

The rain is stingy with the chill
it brings with the summer thunder.
Some's for the trees. Some is for us.
Some's for the cherries on the stalls.

The boiling starts in the dusk
with the light fussing of teapots,
as if some anthill in the sky
were feasting upon dark shoots.

Out of the fresh drops, a vineyard
begins to stir in the grass,
a seedbed of coldness revealed
in Moscow, spread like a palm.

1922

[Untitled]

Voronezh, Crow-Town, when can I go?
You run me to the verge, preserve my knowledge,
rent me a niche, make me veer near the edge,
Voronezh, random, ruining town of crows.

April 1935

Notes on Contributors

JUANA ADCOCK is a poet and translator working in English and Spanish. Her work has appeared in publications such as *Magma Poetry*, *Gutter*, *Glasgow Review of Books*, *Asymptote* and *Words Without Borders*. Her first book, *Manca*, explores the anatomy of violence in Mexico and was considered by *Reforma*'s distinguished critic Sergio González Rodríguez as one of the best poetry books published in 2014.

ASTRID ALBEN's most recent collection *Ai! Ai! Pianissimo* was published by Arc in 2011. Her poems, essays, translations and reviews are widely published in journals, magazines, newspapers and anthologies, and her poetry is translated into several languages. Alben is the editor of three art-science anthologies: *Findings on Ice* (2007), *Findings on Elasticity* (2010) and *Findings on Light* (2015), published by Lars Müller Publications. Her next collection, *Plainspeak*, an alter-ego-thinker-out-louder book, will be ready this year. Alben is a Royal Society of Arts Fellow and Wellcome Trust Fellow. To hear her poems visit www.astridalben.com.

IAN BRINTON is reviews editor for the magazine,*Tears in the Fence*, and is also a widely-published translator and critic. For Shearsman Books he has edited collections of essays on J.H. Prynne and Peter Hughes, and has a further Prynne volume in development.

CARMEN BUGAN is the author of the internationally acclaimed memoir *Burying the Typewriter: Childhood Under the Eye of the Secret Police*, the collections of poems *Crossing the Carpathians* and *The House of Straw*, and the monograph *Seamus Heaney and East European Poetry in Translation: Poetics of Exile*. She also presented the BBC documentary *The Man Who Went Looking for Freedom*, about visiting her father's prisons in Romania.

CLAIRE CROWTHER's recent poetry collections are *On Narrowness* (Shearsman Books, 2015) and the chapbook, *Silents* (Hercules Editions, 2015). She is poet in residence at the Royal Mint Museum for 2014-2015.

IAN DAVIDSON has three collections from Shearsman Books, the most recent being *Partly in Riga, and other poems* (2010).

The Chilean poet Luisa Victoria Anabalón Sanderson (1894-1951) published her mid- and late-career work under the name WINÉTT DE ROKHA. Born to a patrician Catholic family in Santiago, in 1916 she married the poet and communist Pablo de Rokha, a modernist firebrand widely considered to be one of the most important figures in twentieth-century Chilean poetry. Under Pablo's literary influence, Winétt moved away from the fin-de-siècle metrical forms of her early career to write imagistic, syntactically irregular free verse with surrealist, existentialist, even "neo-baroque" qualities. The poems translated here are from *Cantoral* (1936). Her collected work was published posthumously in *Suma y destino* (1951). Over the last decade there has been a renewal of literary and scholarly interest in her poetic achievement, quite independent of her husband's fame. See *Fotografía en oscuro*, a selected edition (Madrid: Colección Torremozas, 2008); and *El valle pierde su atmósfera*, a critical, collected edition (Santiago: Propio Cuarto, 2008).

MARK DICKINSON's first full-length collection, *Tender Geometries*, was published by Shearsman Books in 2015.

CLAYTON ESHLEMAN's poem is the concluding one in a new collection called *Penetralia*, to be published by Black Widow Press in 2016. This fall Black Widow Press is publishing *Clayton Eshleman / The Essential Poetry 1960-2015*. His website is: www.claytoneshleman.com

GERRIE FELLOWS' most recent collection is *The Body in Space* (Shearsman Books 2014). Other work includes two book-length sequences, *Window for a Small Blue Child* and *The Powerlines*. Her poetry can be found at www.gerriefellows.co.uk. She lives and works in Glasgow.

SAMIR GUGLANI is a writer of poetry and short fiction. He completed an MSt in Creative Writing with distinction through Oxford University in 2014. His poem 'X-ray' was a winner of the Radcliffe Library Parallel Universe competition in 2013. He is currently writing a collection of linked short stories around events in a single hospital. He is a consultant oncologist and curator of *Medicine Unboxed*, a project that explores medicine through the arts. He lives and works in Cheltenham.

LUCY HAMILTON co-edits *Long Poem Magazine* and teaches freelance. Her collection *Stalker* (Shearsman, 2012) was shortlisted for the Forward Prizes' Felix Dennis Prize for Best First Collection. In a recent commissioned project, poems from 'The Diarists' sequence were exhibited at the The Scott Polar Museum, Cambridge from November 2014 – March 2015, and appeared in *PN Review* 220. Other poems from her second collection-in-progress have appeared in *Shearsman* 93 & 94, *Her Wings of Glass* (SLP anthology), *PN Review* 211, *Tears in the Fence*, *Molly Bloom* and *Litmus*.

LEE HARWOOD passed away in July 2015 at the age of 76, after contributing the poem in this issue—which is therefore his last, or at least one of his last, poems. His available books are *Collected Poems* (Shearsman Books, 2004), *Selected Poems* (Shearsman, 2008), and *The Orchid Boat* (Enitharmon, 2014). Shearsman also publishes a volume of interviews with him by the editor of this issue, Kelvin Corcoran (*Not the Full Story*, 2008).

PHILIPPE JACCOTTET, born 1925 in Switzerland, has lived in Provence since 1953. One of the finest post-war Francophone poets, he is one of the very few writers to be included in the canonical Bibliothèque de la Pléiade while still living.

DOROTHY LEHANE is the author of *Ephemeris* (Nine Arches Press) and *Places of Articulation* (dancing girl press), both in 2014. She is the founding editor of Litmus Publishing and teaches Creative Writing at the University of Kent.

ANGELA LIVINGSTONE studied Russian and German at Cambridge. From 1966 to 1997 she taught literature (mainly Russian) at the University of Essex, and is now retired as professor emeritus. She has published numerous articles on the work of Pasternak, Tsvetaeva and Platonov, as well as three books about Pasternak (most recently *The Marsh of Gold, Pasternak's Writings on Inspiration and Creation*, Academic Studies Press, 2008); and three books (translations with commentaries) about Tsvetaeva (*Art in the Light of Conscience: Eight Essays by Tsvetaeva on Poetry*; *The Ratcatcher, a Lyrical Satire*; and *Phaedra*, a drama in verse, with the long poems 'New Year's Letter', 'Poem of the Air', and 'Attempt at a Room').

OSIP MANDELSTAM (1891-1938), who fell afoul of Stalin in the 1930s and died in a transit camp on his way to imprisonment in the Gulag, was one of the greatest Russian poets of the 20th century. Initially associated with the Acmeists, he wrote the movement's manifesto. He published two collections during his own lifetime, as well as memoirs, essays and other prose, but the majority of his work was memorised by his widow, Nadezhda, and thus preserved, to be published only following the artistic thaw of the 1960s.

DAVID MILLER was born in Melbourne, Australia, in 1950, and has lived in London since 1972. His more recent publications include *Reassembling Still: Collected Poems* (Shearsman Books, 2014). *Spiritual Letters (Series 1-5)* appeared from Chax Press in 2011 and *(Series 6)* appeared a chapbook from Shearsman Books in 2015. He is also a musician and a member of the Frog Peak Music collective.

HELEN MOORE is an award-winning ecopoet and socially engaged artist. Her debut poetry collection, *Hedge Fund, and Other Living Margins* (Shearsman Books, 2012), was described by Alasdair Paterson as being "in the great tradition of visionary politics in British poetry." Her second collection, *ECOZOA* (Permanent Publications 2015), responds to Thomas Berry's vision of the 'Ecozoic Era', where we live in harmony "with the Earth as community", and has already been acclaimed by John Kinsella as "a milestone in the journey of ecopoetics".

ALISTAIR NOON has two collections from Nine Arches Press, *Earth Records* (2012) and *Bockwurst Halal* (2015). Also due out soon is a collaboration with Giles Goodland (*Surveyors' Riddles*, Sidekick Books). A full-length collection of his widely-published translations of Osip Mandelstam is in preparation. He lives in Berlin.

SABIYHA RASHEED is a recent graduate from the University of Kent with a degree in English and American Literature with Creative Writing. Sabiyha is a working musician as a singer-songwriter and her involvement in the arts, both with music and literature, has aided her exploration of poetry. She is continuing with a collection of poetry, focusing on her interest in race politics and is soon to be published in the University of Kent's 50th Anniversary Anthology.

PETER RILEY was born into an environment of working people in the Manchester area in 1940 and now lives in retirement in Hebden Bridge, West Yorkshire, having previously lived in the Peak District and Cambridge for many years. He has been a teacher, bookseller, and several other things and is the author of some fifteen books of poetry, and two of prose concerning travel and music. His most recent books are *The Glacial Stairway* (Carcanet 2011) and *Due North* (Shearsman Books, 2015), a book-length poem which was shortlisted for the Forward Prize for Best Collection, 2015. He was awarded a Cholmondeley Prize in 2012. He regularly contributes reviews of new poetry to the website *The Fortnightly Review*.

JAIME ROBLES has two collections from Shearsman Books, *Anime Animus Anima* (2010) and *Hoard* (2013).

IAN SEED's collections from Shearsman Books are *Makers of Empty Dreams* (2014), *Shifting Registers* (2011) and *Anonymous Intruder* (2009). His work appears in Salt's *Best British Poetry 2014* (ed. Mark Ford).

AIDAN SEMMENS is editor of the online magazine *Molly Bloom* (mollybloom.org.uk). His third full-length collection, *Uncertain Measures*, was published by Shearsman Books in 2014.

LUCY SHEERMAN lives in Cambridge and is the Chief Executive of the John Clare Cottage Trust and an artist-in-residence at Metal, Peterborough. She is the author of *Rarefied (falling without landing)* from Oystercatcher Press and also appeared in the Shearsman anthology *Infinite Difference* in 2010.

J. MARK SMITH's first book of poetry was *Notes for a Rescue Narrative* (Lantzville, B.C.: Oolichan, 2007). His poem 'Sweetness' was anthologized in the Tightrope Books anthology *Best Canadian Poetry in English* 2008. His work has been published most recently in *Vallum*, *The Malahat Review*, *The Fiddlehead*, *The Antigonish Review*, and *Zócalo Public Square*. He has taught in the English Department at MacEwan University in Edmonton, Alberta since 2006.

DONNA STONECIPHER is the author of four collections, most recently *Model City* (Shearsman Books, 2015).

JANET SUTHERLAND lives in Lewes, East Sussex. She has three collections of poetry from Shearsman Books, the most recent being *Bone Monkey* (2014).

PHILIP TERRY is currently Director of the Centre for Creative Writing at the University of Essex. Among his books are the lipogrammatic novel *The Book of Bachelors*, the edited story collection *Ovid Metamorphosed*, a translation of Raymond Queneau's last book of poems *Elementary Morality*, and the poetry volumes *Oulipoems*, *Oulipoems 2*, *Shakespeare's Sonnets*, and *Advanced Immorality*. His novel *tapestry* was shortlisted for the 2013 Goldsmith's Prize. *Dante's Inferno*, which relocates Dante's action to current day Essex, was published in 2014.

HELEN TOOKEY lives in Liverpool and teaches creative writing at Liverpool John Moores University. Her first full-length collection, *Missel-Child*, was published by Carcanet in 2014 and has been shortlisted for the 2015 Seamus Heaney Centre for Poetry prize for a first collection.

The life of MARINA TSVETAEVA (1892-1941), now recognised as a major Russian, and indeed European, poet of the 20th century, was marked to an unusual extent by the political and ideological conflicts of her time. Born to a privileged background in Moscow, the revolutions of 1917 brought her crushing hardship and deprivation, but also ushered in a period of unparalleled creativity as poet and playwright. In 1922 she left for the west to rejoin her husband, who had fought with the counter-revolutionary forces. In 1925 the family moved from near Prague to Paris. Their existence was marked by appalling poverty and a growing alienation from the Russian émigré community. When in 1937 her husband was implicated in an assassination carried out by the Stalinist secret services, Tsvetaeva saw no alternative but to follow him back to the USSR. After the Nazis invaded Russia, she was evacuated to Yelabuga, where she took her own life in August 1941. Shearsman Books has recently published her 1922 volume, *Milestones*, in Christopher Whyte's translation.

ELŻBIETA WÓJCIK-LEESE is a writer, translator and scholar who moves between English, Polish and Danish. Her recent publications include *Metropoetica. Poetry and Urban Space: Women Writing Cities* (collaborative project between 6 languages; Seren, 2013) and *Nothing More* (translations of Krystyna Miłobędzka, Arc Publications, 2013).

AMY WRIGHT is the Nonfiction Editor of Zone 3 Press, and the author of five chapbooks. Her work appears in *Brevity, DIAGRAM, Southern Poetry Anthology* (Volumes III and VI), *Quarterly West, Tupelo Quarterly, Kenyon Review*, and can be found online at awrightawright.com

TAMAR YOSELOFF's most recent collections are *The City with Horns* (Salt Publishing, 2011) and *Formerly*, a chapbook incorporating photographs by Vici MacDonald (Hercules Editions, 2012), which was shortlisted for the 2012 Ted Hughes Award. *A Formula for Night: New and Selected Poems* is due from Seren in October 2015.

www.ingramcontent.com/pod-product-compliance
Lightning Source LLC
Chambersburg PA
CBHW030957090426
42737CB00007B/577